Dinosaurs
and me

DK Publishing

LONDON, NEW YORK, MUNICH,
MELBOURNE and DELHI

Written by Marie Greenwood
Designed by Victoria Harvey
Consultant David Burnie

Design development manager Helen Senior
Publishing manager Bridget Giles
Category publisher Sue Leonard
Production Rita Sinha
Production editor Marc Staples
Index by Chris Bernstein

First American Edition, 2011
Published in the United States by
DK Publishing
375 Hudson Street
New York, New York 10014

11 12 13 14   10 9 8 7 6 5 4 3 2 1

001–179429–September/2011

Published in Great Britain by Dorling Kindersley Limited.

A catalog record for this book is available from the Library of Congress.

ISBN 978-0-7566-8603-1
DK books are available at special discounts when purchased in bulk for
sales promotions, premiums, fund-raising, or educational use. For details,
contact: DK Publishing Special Markets, 375 Hudson Street, New York,
New York 10014 or SpecialSales@dk.com.

Printed and bound in China by Toppan Printing Co. Ltd.

Discover more at
www.dk.com

Contents

Early reptiles

Dinosaurs were among the first reptiles to walk on Earth. They had scaly skin, like most of today's reptiles. The name "dinosaur" means "terrible lizard."

Walk tall

Dinosaurs had four legs, although many walked upright on two, just like we do. Although dinosaurs have disappeared, there are still lots of four-legged animals.

Fossilized remains found in rocks show us what dinosaurs looked like.

Most amphibians, such as frogs, have four legs. They live partly in water, partly on land.

swish!

Tortoises move very slowly on their four legs. Their hard shells help protect them from being eaten.

Lizards and most other reptiles have legs that spread out sideways, with their bodies close to the ground.

I'm a reptile!

flap! flap!

This is what the world would have looked like 65 million years ago. The continents were slowly taking shape, and the dinosaur age was nearing its end.

hello!

Birds look very different than dinosaurs, but they are in fact closely related. For one thing, they both lay eggs.

Like dinosaurs, we walk on two legs. This leaves our arms free for lifting and holding things.

Dinosaurs walked upright, keeping their bodies off the ground.

Most dinosaurs had long tails, which helped them to keep their balance when running.

T. rex's head was about as long as a fully-grown human.

ROar!

A tall story

We always think of dinosaurs as being huge, but they weren't all big. Some were about the size of a chicken. Others were the same size as us.

How big were they?

While it's true that dinosaurs varied in size, it's the big ones that we hear about the most. The giant meat-eating *Tyrannosaurus rex* (meaning "lizard king"), or *T. rex*, must be the most famous of them all.

Lesothosaurus was one of the smallest dinosaurs and could run very fast.

I'm the smallest!

Whoosh!

I'm the tallest!

Quetzalcoatlus was the biggest of the flying reptiles. Its wingspan was about three times wider than an albatross's.

Me!

A human's hands are at least half the size of *Troodon*'s claws.

Dino!

Liopleurodon was the biggest aquatic reptile, half the size of the blue whale, at 50 ft (16 m).

Animal!

The blue whale is bigger than any dinosaur at 108 ft (33 m).

Troodon was just a bit taller than you and me. It was pretty brainy, too—for a dinosaur. It was about as smart as a modern bird.

Sauropods were the tallest animals that have ever lived. Some were more than twice the height of a giraffe.

hello!

Skeleton
shapes

Although you might

not think it at first, dinosaur skeletons are rather like our own. They gave dinosaurs their shape and protected their insides from harm—just like our skeletons do.

I've got two legs...

Many dinosaurs such as *Tyrannosaurus rex* walked on two upright legs like we do. Their bones were light in weight—perfect for running fast.

Airy bones

Most meat-eating dinosaurs had bones filled with air. Though their bones were huge, they weren't as heavy as they looked. Birds today have the same kind of hollow bones.

Me!
The smallest bones in your skeleton are inside your ears.

Dino!
Apatosaurus's thigh bone was taller than an adult man.

Animal!
Sharks have rubbery, rather than bony, skeletons

Where's the sunscreen?

Ouranosaurus had long bones sticking out of its back. They were covered in skin, and helped it keep warm in the sun.

...and me!

Your skeleton is made up of 206 bones. They are light in weight to help you move easily and quickly.

Baby Mussaurus are the smallest dinosaur skeletons ever found. They would fit inside a shopping bag!

Crocodiles and other reptiles are different than dinosaurs in that their legs stick out on either side.

...I walk on four!

Carcharodontosaurus's skull had large openings, which made it light. This dinosaur could swallow a person in one bite.

gulp!

Bone head

Some dinosaurs had enormous heads, but very small brains. They weren't dumb, though. They could still keep out of danger and find food.

Dino IQ

Some dinosaurs were brighter than others. Small meat eaters were the smartest, and often hunted in packs. *Stegosaurus* (right) wasn't so bright. It didn't need to be. Its diet of plants was easy to find.

pea brain!

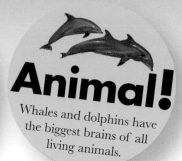
butt out!

Edmontosaurus

was one of the many dinosaurs that had a mouth shaped like a duck's beak.

Pachycephalosaurus (left) had an extra-thick dome on the top of its head. It might have been used to headbutt, like goats do today.

eye eye!

Our eyes face forward, so we can see in 3D. The eyes of plant-eating dinosaurs like *Triceratops* looked out to each side, so they could watch for danger while they fed.

I can see you...

Triceratops had the biggest skull with a solid shield of any dinosaur. It was up to 6½ ft (2 m) long, with a bony shield over its neck.

Cover up

Most dinosaurs had scaly skin, like lizards and snakes. Our skin is very different. It is soft and stretchy, and covered with millions of hairs.

Some dinosaurs may have had colorful skins, but no one knows for sure. Most probably had green and brown scales to help them hide behind trees and plants.

Scaly skin

This type of skin is tough and waterproof. It protected dinosaurs from injury, and helped stop them from drying out.

can you see me?

Snakes and lizards shed their skin so that they can grow. Dinosaurs may have done this too. A snake's skin sometimes comes off in one piece, like a sock being pulled inside out.

I'm tough!

Dinosaur scales were often made of added layers (reinforced) to make them strong.

Me!

Your skin grows all the time, so it can wear down without wearing out.

Animal!

Many frogs and toads can breathe through their skin.

Dino!

Newly hatched dinosaurs had soft, slippery scales that soon dried out.

look at me!

Corythosaurus may have had a colorful crest on its head. It used this to attract attention from a possible mate.

Saltasaurus was one of the biggest reinforced dinosaurs—it had bony plates and bumps scattered over its back.

bumpy!

Mammals are the only animals that have hair. Your hair grows on average about 0.01 in (3 mm) a week.

Some dinosaurs had bony plates, others had bumps, and some even had spikes.

hoofy!

handy!

Iguanodon's feet had hooves, a bit like a pig's. It usually got down on all fours to feed.

T. rex had huge back legs, but its tiny front legs were not much longer than human arms.

Deinonychus's legs ended in razor-sharp swivelling claws that were 10 in (25 cm) long.

Leggy lizards

Dinosaurs had four legs, but some ran on two and others switched between two and four, like a car changing gear.

Big feet

Dinosaurs had the same set of leg bones, but some had feet like a rhinoceros or an elephant. Others had feet like a bird. The biggest footprints found were 3 ft (1 m) across.

Dinosaur footprints sometimes turned fossils.

I'm well armed...

I'm a softy...

Therizinosaurus had gigantic claws on its hands, up to 3 ft (1 m) long.

Megalosaurus had huge back legs and feet with three forward-pointing toes.

Sauropods had big, round cushiony feet which helped bear their massive weight.

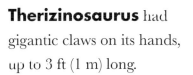

Me!
The biggest muscles in your body are in your legs.

Dino!
Big dinosaurs may have stayed standing up, since they had trouble getting up from the ground.

Animal!
Millipedes have more legs than any other animal—up to 750.

We have nimble fingers which allow us to make fine, delicate movements and to grip things tightly. Some dinosaurs also had flexible fingers, which they used to pick up their food.

flexy!

Feeling hungry

Dinosaurs ate all kinds of things, just like wild animals do today.
Some were meat eaters, but many fed on plants.

fishing...

Dinosaur teeth

Dinosaurs had very different teeth than we do.
They were specially shaped to tackle their favorite food.
Many had teeth that grew nonstop. When a tooth wore
away, it dropped out, and a new one took its place.

Suchomimus had jaws
and teeth like a crocodile's so
that slippery fish could not
get away easily.

Large stones were often
swallowed by dinosaurs. These
stayed in the stomach, and helped
them grind up their food.

Oviraptor was a strange looking
dinosaur with a bird-like beak. It
did not have any teeth at all.

We have two sets of teeth.
Our milk teeth come first.
They are replaced by a second
set, called permanent teeth.

eggy!

toothy!

beaky!

Gallimimus liked
an egg for breakfast
just like we do!

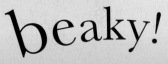

Me!

Some people are vegetarians, like many dinosaurs were.

Dino!

T. rex ate up to 22 tons (20 tonnes) of meat a year.

Animal!

Some snakes can go a whole year between meals.

rip!

Plant-eating dinosaurs, like *Brachiosaurus*, bit off, or tore off, their food, with teeth that worked like garden rakes.

Hyenas feed on dead remains of other animals, much like some hunting dinosaurs did. They used their sense of smell to find their food.

I'm hungry!

T. rex was a terrifying hunter with jagged teeth 6 in (15 cm) long. Unlike us, it couldn't chew, so it swallowed its food in enormous chunks. *T. rex* was huge—it weighed more than an elephant.

Attack!

Bigger than wolves, and almost as smart, *Velociraptor* hunted in packs. But unlike wolves, they were agile enough to jump on their victim's back.

Run!

Jump!

Hunting

Meat-eating dinosaurs launched deadly attacks on their prey, much like many wild animals do today. Smaller hunters often worked together in packs.

Ambushed!

The biggest hunters were too slow to chase their prey. They quietly stalked their victims, attacking by surprise. Some dinosaurs were cannibals and ate their own kind.

swish

Me!

Human hunters have helped to make some animals, like the dodo, extinct.

Dino!

Hunters had to eat quickly, before bigger dinosaurs arrived.

Animal!

The Komodo dragon lizard is a cannibal, like some dinosaurs were.

Come on!

Hunting dinosaurs didn't all eat big prey. Some of the smallest kinds fed on lizards and flying insects, snatched out of the air.

I can see you!

Deinosuchus was a massive prehistoric crocodile. It probably had a stronger bite than any of the dinosaurs, including *T. rex*. It weighed eight times as much as today's crocodiles.

Troodon had extra large eyes to seek out its prey at night.

Talking
about it

Most living reptiles don't make sounds, but dinosaurs may have used sounds to keep in touch, stay together, and warn if danger was on its way.

How loud were they?

We don't really know how much noise dinosaurs made. But the loudest sounds might have carried more than 15 ½ miles (25 km).

Corythosaurus had a big hollow crest connected to its nose. The crest worked like an echo chamber, letting it make a deafening blast of sound.

rumble rumble!

chubby…

…cheeks!

Plant-eating dinosaurs made lots of noises as they digested their food, just like elephants do.

If you blow into a trumpet, you puff your cheeks out. *Corythosaurus* may have used its cheeks to make sounds in much the same way.

musical!

Plant eaters may have stamped their feet to warn of danger or to keep dinosaur hunters away.

Parasaurolophus had a crest shaped like half a trombone. The male's was up to 6 ft (1.8 m) long—the biggest in the dinosaur world.

Me!
People use over 4,000 different languages across the world.

Animal!
The howler monkey is the loudest animal on land.

Dino!
Some baby dinosaurs may have cheeped inside their eggs.

Stomping!

Struthiomimus, along with other small hunters, probably made high-pitched, screechy noises, rather like an ostrich. Its name means "ostrich mimic."

screech!

On the move

Imagine a race between dinosaurs, today's animals, and people. Dinosaurs might not do as well as you would think. Many were slow movers, held back by their size and weight. The cheetah would have beaten them all.

Ready, set, go!

come on!

T. rex

Ankylosaurus

Sauropods

Stegosaurus

Athlete

Slowest

Some huge dinosaurs had short legs, so they could not run very fast. Other slow movers included those with big, heavy plates, such as *Stegosaurus*.

While we are flat-footed, dinosaurs, cats, and dogs walk on their toes.

Feathered friends

Bird-like dinosaurs, such as *Velociraptor*, were fast and agile. They had long, slender back legs and light bodies. They used their short, feathery arms to help them run faster.

Dino!
Dinosaurs that ran on two legs were called bipeds.

Me!
T. rex may have run as fast as a person—about 18 mph (28 km/h).

Animal!
Antelopes could match the speed of the fastest dinosaurs.

ZOOOOom!

Velociraptor

Racehorse

Ostrich

Compsognathus

Ornithomimus

Cheetah

Winner!

Fastest

Slim, lizard-like dinosaurs, such as *Compsognathus* and *Ornithomimus*, were among the fastest dinosaurs. They used their tails for balance.

head lock!

Triceratops had three enormous horns, up to 3 ft (1 m) long. It used its horns to fight its rivals, and also to fend off attack.

Self defense

Dinosaurs needed to defend themselves from possible attack, just like animals today protect themselves from their enemies.

Keep back!

Dinosaurs had different methods of self-defense. Meat eaters had sharp teeth. Some plant eaters had long horns or sharp spikes. Others were covered in bony plates.

The armadillo is protected by a tough, plated shell, like some dinosaurs once were.

beaky!

Protoceratops protected itself by biting enemies with its sharp beak.

Ankylosaurus fought its enemies with its bony, club-ended tail, sometimes smashing the attacker's skull.

Swish!

Me!
Football players wear their own "armor" to protect themselves.

Dino!
Corythosaurus had a crest shaped like a soldier's helmet.

Animal!
Tortoises have their own special armor— their shells.

Red deer fight each other by locking antlers. They do this to compete for a mate, just like *Triceratops* did.

Show offs

Male dinosaurs needed to attract females to mate with. They were natural show offs, like many male animals today.

Frills and thrills

To help them stand out from the crowd, some male dinosaurs had colorful body parts. They may also have competed in tests of strength.

Chameleons change color to show their mood. Some dinosaurs may have done just the same thing.

Stegosaurus had huge upright plates on its back. Males might have made them change color or "blush" to catch a female's eye.

Hi!

Chasmosaurus had a huge head shield or "frill" made of skin. This may have been brightly colored to help it attract a mate.

frilly!

Tigers live mainly alone and come together just to mate. In the same way, big dinosaur hunters, such as *T. rex*, met to breed, then went their separate ways.

Dino!
Most dinosaurs had babies just once a year.

Me!
People use clothes to attract attention, like other animals use feathers or fur.

Animal!
Male birds of paradise are among the biggest show offs.

hello!

Hatching

Dinosaurs built nests and laid eggs, like birds and reptiles do today. Some fed and protected their babies, helping them to survive.

Dinosaur babies

On first hatching, dinosaur babies were small and helpless. Their parents sometimes took care of them until they were big enough to leave the nest.

Hello babies!

Some dinosaur eggs looked like ostrich eggs (left). *Protoceratops'* eggs (center) were thinner, while Sauropod eggs (right) were more rounded.

Maiasaura made large, rounded nests out of earth, with about 30 to 40 eggs laid in circles— like the nests of today's seabirds. The eggs were about the same size as ostrich eggs. *Maiasaura* means "good mother lizard."

A human baby stays close to its mother for the first few years of its life. Some dinosaurs, such as *Maiasaura*, cared for their young until they were old enough to fend for themselves.

Gather round chicks!

Me!

Humans give birth to live young, like all mammals do.

Dino!

The earliest dinosaur eggs to be discovered were at first thought to belong to giant birds.

The families of emperor penguins are made up of a few adults caring for large numbers of chicks. Some dinosaurs, such as *Psittacosaurus*, may have cared for their young in a similar way.

Animal!

Some turtles lay their eggs through tubes, like giant sauropods may have done.

Mommy!

Some dinosaurs could run soon after they had hatched, often to escape from predators. This is like the babies of today's mammals, such as zebras and gazelles.

Buffalo move in huge herds on Africa's open plains. In the same way, plant-eating dinosaurs lived in herds of over a thousand.

On the move...

Dinosaur herds moved, or migrated, away from cold weather, or toward good places to feed— just like today's animal herds.

Sticking together

Coelophysis followed plant-eating herds and hunted any young or sick animals that strayed.

Plant-eating dinosaurs often lived together for protection, just like herding animals do today. These herds contained either a handful of adults and their young, or many thousands of animals.

Sauropods could travel many miles a day on their huge legs. Their fossilized "trackways," or "superhighways," can still be seen today.

follow me!

Me!
Like many dinos, humans are naturally sociable and like to stick together!

Dino!
Dinosaur herds did everything together, from feeding and drinking to migrating and laying eggs.

Animal!
Musk oxen protect their young by forming a ring, like *Triceratops* did.

Safety in numbers

Living in a herd is a good way to keep safe. While most herd members feed, others are on the lookout. They sound the alarm if anything dangerous comes near.

Fossils of an *Iguanodon* herd were found deep underground by miners in Belgium. They included adults and their young.

Bats have wings made of skin, like pterosaurs did. But unlike bats, they use four fingers to keep their wings outstretched.

SWOOP!

Pterodaustro had a bristly beak, like a brush. It probably fed in shallow water, scooping up tiny animals in this sieve-like beak.

Quetzalcoatlus was bigger than many small airplanes, with two wings about 39 ft (12 m) from tip to tip.

Taking flight

At the time of the dinosaurs, flying reptiles—called pterosaurs—flew through the skies. Their wings were made of skin, held out by long finger bones.

How big were they?

Some pterosaurs were not much bigger than a chicken, but the largest were three times the size of any bird today. *Quetzalcoatlus* was longer than many dinosaurs, but it probably weighed less than two adult men.

Screech!

Most pterosaurs were probably covered in fuzzy fur, which would have kept them warm.

Eudimorphodon had a big toothy beak and a long bony tail. Its wings were held open by a very slim fourth finger.

Rhamphorhynchus sometimes crashed into the sea when looking for fish. Its pointed beak and sticking-out teeth helped it catch slippery food.

Dino!
Some small dinosaurs, such as *Microraptor*, had feathers and could glide, but not fly.

Animal!
The hoatzin bird has claws on its wings, just like a pterosaur.

Me!
Humans can't fly, but with the help of a harness and fabric "wing," they can paraglide.

WOOsh...!

Dimorphodon had a chunky beak, like a puffin's. It probably lived near the sea and fed on fish.

Sea turtles were a favorite food of the alligator-like *Deinosuchus*.

In the deep

Giant reptiles and fish

swam in the deep blue seas in prehistoric times, at the same time that dinosaurs walked on land. Alongside these big sea creatures, lived jellyfish, squid, and turtles.

Elasmosaurus was a giant, air-breathing reptile, in some ways like today's whales, though its neck was about 23 ft (7 m) long.

Pterygotus was a huge sea scorpion that attacked its victims with its giant pincers .... watch out—it could grow to be much longer than you!

snap! snap!

swim away!

yum yum!

Me!
We can swim at speeds up to 5.3 mph (8.5 km/h)—about the same as Steller's sea cow, an extinct sea mammal.

Dino!
Megalodon tooth

Megalodon was the biggest prehistoric fish. It looked like a shark, though it was three times bigger.

Animal!
The earliest turtles lived at the time of the first dinosaurs—about 215 million years ago.

Baryonyx lived near the water and used its mighty claws as hooks to catch fish. It gripped its food with its huge crocodile-like jaws.

Ichthyosaurus was a reptile whose name means "fish lizard," though it really looked more like a shark.

Present-day shark

Jellyfish have been around for 400 million years—even before the dinosaurs.

Deinosuchus looked like a crocodile or alligator, but it was twice as big—it was about 40 ft (12 m). Its name means "terrible crocodile."

Present-day crocodile

Early mammals

Megazostrodon

Alongside the dinosaurs lived all kinds of mammals. These small, quick-moving hunters searched for food mainly at night.

Time of the dinosaurs

Early mammals varied a lot from dinosaurs. They were much smaller, and they had fur, which helped their bodies keep warm.

Megazostrodon was one of the earliest mammals. It was about the size of a mouse.

Squeek!

ZZZZZZZZZZZZZZZZZZZzzz

Dinosaurs and other reptiles slow down in cold weather, but mammals could keep looking for food.

After the dinosaurs

Once dinosaurs died out, the world changed. Mammals grew bigger and it was their turn to rule.

Protorohippus was one of the very first horses. It was about the size of a small dog.

Paraceratherium was the biggest ever land mammal. It was related to the rhino.

Me!
You have four types of teeth, just like the first mammals did.

Dino!
The dinosaurs died out when a giant meteor hit the Earth, but mammals survived.

Animal!
When scientists first saw a duck-billed platypus, they thought it was a joke!

Squeal....

Glub!

Early mammals fed on their mother's milk, just like mammals, such as these baby piglets, do today.

Sinodelphys's young grew up in the safety of their mother's pouch— much like baby kangaroos do.

Steropon had a beak like a duck and laid eggs instead of giving birth. It is related to today's duck-billed platypus.

Smilodon was a tiger-like cat with huge front teeth. They were so big, they stuck out when its mouth was closed.

The woolly mammoth had long fur, making it well suited to living in frozen northern lands.

Grrr!

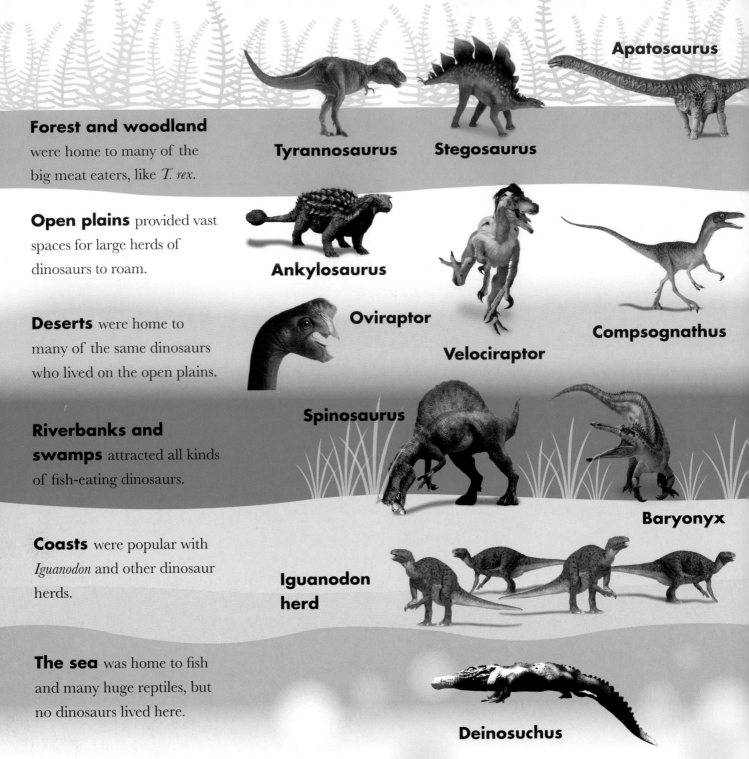

Forest and woodland were home to many of the big meat eaters, like *T. rex*.

Tyrannosaurus

Stegosaurus

Apatosaurus

Open plains provided vast spaces for large herds of dinosaurs to roam.

Ankylosaurus

Oviraptor

Velociraptor

Compsognathus

Deserts were home to many of the same dinosaurs who lived on the open plains.

Riverbanks and swamps attracted all kinds of fish-eating dinosaurs.

Spinosaurus

Baryonyx

Coasts were popular with *Iguanodon* and other dinosaur herds.

Iguanodon herd

The sea was home to fish and many huge reptiles, but no dinosaurs lived here.

Deinosuchus

Where they lived

Like today's world, the prehistoric one was full of different habitats, or homes, where dinosaurs could live—from dry desert to lush, green forests.

Diplodocus

Maiasaura

Brachiosaurus

Therizinosaurus

Quetzalcoatlus

Dromaeosaurus

Ornithomimus

Ouranosaurus

Carcharodontosaurus

screech!

Suchomimus

Pterodactylus

Ichthyosaurus

Elasmosaurus

Me!
Humans are the only animals that live everywhere, except under the sea.

Dino!
Dinosaurs that lived near water often left the best preserved fossils.

Animal!
Marine iguanas are the only lizards that feed in the sea.

Plant life

Many weird and wonderful plants grew at the time of the dinosaurs. Ferns grew as high as houses, and palm-shaped cycads grew prickly leaves.

Hot and steamy

Before dinosaurs arrived on Earth, the weather was often hot and steamy—just right for forests to grow.

Dinosaurs fed on the hard woody cones of evergreen coniferous trees.

munch! munch!

The broad leaves of the maidenhair tree, or ginkgo, have hardly changed since the time of the dinosaurs.

Cycads were among the most common plants. Dinosaurs needed strong teeth and stomachs to feed on their tough, prickly leaves.

Me!

Tiny pollen grains from flowers can make you sneeze!

Giant dragonflies

fluttered among the trees long before dinosaurs arrived.

Animal!

Early insects spread their pollen, just as they do today.

Dino!

Platybelodon, a prehistoric elephant, shoveled up plants with its spade-like tusks.

flutter by!

The first flowers looked

like magnolias. They were pollinated by beetles, since they appeared before bees had arrived on Earth.

Plants and fungi

grew on Earth long before dinosaurs were around. Some had very strange shapes.

Fly away!

Some birds today, such as swifts, stay in the air for years. They even eat and sleep in the air.

Archaeopteryx was one of the earliest birds, with a toothy beak and a long bony tail.

Birds have fewer, smaller bones than dinosaurs, which help them fly.

Where they fit in

Dinosaurs and other prehistoric animals did not disappear without trace. They are related to birds and today's reptiles, such as crocodiles.

Early bird

Amazingly, birds are descended from dinosaurs, even though some of them are tiny. The smallest of all is the bee humingbird.

The bee hummingbird is 2 in (5 cm) long—smaller than many butterflies.

Today's reptiles include snakes and lizards. All of them have scaly skin, just like dinosaurs.

Let's clap cousin!

Tortoises were among the earliest reptiles. Their hard shells protected them from predators.

Chimpanzees are our closest living relatives. They make faces and clap hands like we do.

Me!
Chimps have their own fingerprints, just like me or you!

Dino!
The dinosaurs died out over 60 million years before humans first appeared.

Animal!

Our prehistoric ancestors lived in Africa, long after the dinosaurs died out. Unlike other animals, they learned how to hunt with stone tools. They also learned how to make fire, which helped keep them warm.

Record holders

Dinosaurs included the biggest animals that have ever lived on land, as well as the fastest and most dangerous. Which is your favorite?

Biggest hunter

Spinosaurus—up to 49 ft (15 m) long.

Biggest plant eater

Argentinosaurus—up to 98 ft (30 m) long.

Smallest

Microraptor—just 31 in (80 cm) long.

Tallest plant eater

Brachiosaurus—its head was up to 39 ft (12 m) off the ground.

Thickest skull

Pachycephalosaurus—up to 8 in (20 cm) thick.

Biggest flying reptile

Quetzalcoatlus—wingspan up to 39 ft (12 m).

Longest claws

Therizinosaurus —up to 3 ft (1 m) long.

Tallest hunter

Deinocheirus—head up to 20 ft (6 m) off the ground.

Fastest

Ornithomimus—ran at up to 43½ mph (70 km/h).

Toothiest

Hadrosaurs could have over 1,000 teeth—they kept growing new ones.

Biggest skull

Pentaceratops—up to 10 ft (3 m) long.

Glossary

Amphibian – a cold-blooded animal with thin, moist skin that lives partly on land, partly in water.

Biped – an animal that moves on two feet.

Coniferous – a tree or shrub, which is usually an evergreen, with needle leaves and cones, e.g. pine.

Cycad – a group of evergreen plants found in tropical areas, which are similar to palms and ferns.

Extinct – no longer exists as a species.

Fossil – imprint of ancient plants or animals, usually preserved in rock.

Fungi – mushrooms and moulds. Fungi often look like plants, but grow in a different way, and do not have roots or leaves.

Hadrosaurs – dinosaurs with jaws shaped like a duck's beak.

Herd – a group of animals of the same species, or type.

Mammal – a warm-blooded animal that is covered in fur or hair, breathes with its lungs, and feeds its young milk.

Predator – an animal that hunts another animal in order to kill and eat it.

Prehistoric – anything that happened before human history began.

Prey – an animal that is, or could be, killed and eaten by another animal.

Pterosaurs – a group of flying reptiles, now extinct.

Reptile – a cold-blooded animal that has a dry, scaly skin, and sometimes bony plates.

Sauropods – a group of large, four-legged plant-eating dinosaurs, with bulky bodies, long necks and tails, and tiny heads.

Scales – small, flat, overlapping plates that cover certain animals, e.g. lizards.

Dinosaur names

Here are the dinosaurs and other prehistoric animals that appear in this book, together with a guide to help you pronounce their names.

ɪkylosaurus
(-KIE-loh-SORE-us)

ɔatosaurus
(-PAT-oh-SORE-us)

rchaeopteryx
(r-kee-OP-ter-iks)

gentinosaurus
(r-gen-TEEN-oh-SORE-us)

ɑryonyx
(r-ee-ON-iks)

ɑchiosaurus
(ak-ee-oh-SORE-us)

ɪrcharodontosaurus
(r-kar-oh-DON-to-SORE-us)

ɑasmosaurus
(z-moh-SORE-us)

elophysis
(e-loh-FIE-sis)

mpsognathus
(mp-soh-NAY-thus)

rythosaurus
(h-rith-oh-SORE-us)

ɪinocheirus
(e-noh-KEE-rus)

ɪinosuchus
(e-noh-SUE-kus)

morphodon
(e-MORF-oh-don)

Diplodocus
(dih-PLOH-de-kus)

Dromaeosaurus
(droh-may-oh-SORE-us)

Edmontosaurus
(ed-mon-toh-SORE-us)

Elasmosaurus
(ee-lahz-mow-SORE-us)

Gallimimus
(gal-lee-MEE-mus)

Ichthyosaurus
(ikh-thee-oh-SORE-us)

Iguanodon
(ig-WHAH-noh-don)

Lesothosaurus
(le-soh-toh-SORE-us)

Liopleurodon
(lie-oh-PLOO-roh-don)

Maiasaura
(my-ee-ah-SORE-ah)

Megalodon
(meh-gah-loh-DON)

Megalosaurus
(meh-gah-loh-SORE-us)

Megazostrodon
(meh-gah-zoh-STRO-don)

Microraptor
(my-kro-RAP-tor)

Ornithomimus
(ore-nih-tho-MEE-mus)

Ouranosaurus
(oo-ran-oh-SORE-us)

Oviraptor
(ohv-ih-RAP-tor)

Pachycephalosaurus
(pak-ee-SEF-a-loh-SORE-us)

Paraceratherium
(par-ah-ser-ah-THAIR-ee-um)

Parasaurolophus
(par-ah-SORE-oh-LOAF-us)

Pentaceratops
(pen-tah-SAIR-uh-tops)

Platybelodon
(plat-ee-BEL-oh-don)

Protoceratops
(pro-toe-SAIR-oh-tops)

Protorohippus
(pro-toe-roh-HIP-us)

Psittacosaurus
(si-tak-oh-SORE-us)

Pterodaustro
(ter-roh-DAW-stroh)

Pterygotus
(teh-ree-GOH-tus)

Quetzalcoatlus
(kwet-zal-COAT-lus)

Rhamphorhynchus
(ram-for-RING-khus)

Saltasaurus
(sal-teh-SORE-us)

Sinodelphys
(sin-oh-DELF-ees)

Smilodon
(SMY-lo-don)

Spinosaurus
(spy-noh-SORE-us)

Stegosaurus
(steg-oh-SORE-us)

Steropon
(STEH-roh-pon)

Struthiomimus
(strooth-ee-oh-MEE-mus)

Suchomimus
(sook-oh-MEE-mus)

Therizinosaurus
(thair-uh-ZIN-oh-SORE-us)

Triceratops
(try-SERRA-tops)

Troodon
(TROH-oh-don)

Tyrannosaurus
(tie-RAN-oh-SORE-us)

Velociraptor
(veh-LOSS-ih-rap-tor)

  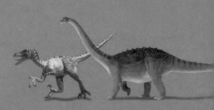

Index

Picture Credits: The publisher would like to thank the following for their kind permission to reproduce their photographs:

(Key: a-above; b-below/bottom; c-centre; f-far; l-left; r-right; t-top)

Alamy Images: Arco Images GmbH / P. Wegner 11tr; blickwinkel / Dautel 23c; Lee Dalton 42br; Encyclopaedia Britannica / Universal Images Group Limited 7cra; Frank Geisler / medicalpicture 9tr; ICP 17tl; imac 9cr; Schulz Ingo / WoodyStock 37ca; Juniors Bildarchiv / R304 23clb; McPhoto / Vario Images GmbH & Co.KG 41fcla; Photoshot Holdings Ltd 7te; Friedrich Saurer / imagebroker 32tr, 45tl; Chris Selby 33crb; Lana Sundman 21ftr; Zach Vanwagner 16cr; Valentyn Volkov 17tla; Louie Psihoyos 21ftr; Dave Watts 37cr; Zee 17tc. **Corbis:** O. Alamany & E. Vicens 17clb; Louie Psihoyos 10t; Louie Psihoyos / Science Faction 9c, 23cr, 39fcra (ornithomimus), 45cr; Hans Reinhard 37tr; Rubberball 13cl; Stuart Westmorland 39br (iguana). **Dorling Kindersley:** Jerry Young 19cl, 19c; Luis V. Rey 23fcl, 38cra; The American Museum of Natural History 8; Bedrock Studios 15ca; Robert L. Braun - modelmaker 3br, 4-5, 6br, 10br, 13cr, 19tc, 22cb, 23cb, 26bl, 38tr, 38fcra; Centaur Studios - modelmaker 14fcla, 24tr, 31fcrb, 35tr; David Donkin - modelmaker 5tr; ESPL 9fbl; Jonathan Hatcley - modelmaker 16fcl, 38cr, 39cl (suchomimus), 42tl; Graham High - modelmaker 2r; Graham High and Jeremy Hunt Centaur Studios - modelmaker 18tl; Graham High at Centaur Studios - modelmaker 13tr, 14tc, 18tr, 20br, 22cla, 22fcr, 23ftr (t-rex), 24tl, 27cb, 27br, 38tc, 39tr (brachiosaurus), 45bl; John Holmes - modelmaker 23tr; John Holmes - modelmaker / Natural History Museum, London 13cla, 28br; Jon Hughes 3tr, 15tr, 27fcra/1, 27fcra/2, 32cl, 33d, 33cl, 37ftr, 38ca, 38c, 39cr (pterodactylus), 39fcla (ouranosaurus), 43c, 44cl; Jon Hughes / Bedrock Studios 15cla, 35cb, 39ftr (therizinosaurus),

45tr; Jeremy Hunt at Centaur Studios - modelmaker 7r, 15c, 30-31ca, 30-31c, 31fcr, 39ftl (barosaurus); Museo Arentino De Cirendas Naterales, Buenos Aires 9bl; Natural History Museum, London 9br, 11cl, 14br, 14fcra, 19cr, 22cl, 28cr, 35cla (tooth), 36bl, 36c, 37bl, 39tc (deinonychus), 43bc, 44br; Paignton Zoo, Devon 7bc; David Peart 35c; Royal Tyrrell Museum of Palaeontology, Alberta, Canada 7cla, 7fbl, 15br; State Museum of Nature, Stuttgart 29cra; Dennis Wilson - Staab Studios - modelmaker 27t; Jerry Young 41cla (butterfly). **Fotolia:** Anna Khomulo 34cr, 35cr; Michael Rosskothen 33ca, 44crb. **Getty Images:** Absodels 22br; The Agency Collection / Clerkenwell 11ftl; Blend Images / Caroline Schiff 20bl; Paul Burns 21fcla; DEA Picture Library 7ca; Digital Vision / Flying Colours 43cra; Flickr / James R. D. Scott 35cra (turtle); Gallo Images / Heinrich van den Berg 23br; Image Source 39fcrb (elasmosaurus); The Image Bank / David Tipling 33cra; The Image Bank / Frans Lemmens 24br; The Image Bank / Siri Stafford 29tr; National Geographic / Jeffrey L. Osborn 45cl; National Geographic / Joel Sartore 34tr; National Geographic / Paul Nicklen 31crb; PhotoAlto / Laurence Mouton 16cl; Photodisc 22fcrb; Photodisc / Bill Reitzel 16bc; Photodisc / Digital Zoo 17cla; Photodisc / Don Farrall 2cr, 40cb, 41cl, 41c, 41clb; Photodisc / Steve Wisbauer 42br (pencil); Photographer's Choice / Blake Little 25fclb; Photographer's Choice / David Young-Wolff 29tl; Photographer's Choice / Martin Ruegner 29ca; Photographer's Choice RF / Sami Sarkis 34cr; Purestock 27cr; Radius Images / Horst Herget 14cra; Riser / David Hall 35fcra; Rubberball / Mike Kemp 13tl (woman); Stock Image / Stefan Meyers 25b; Stone / Michael Blann 43tl; Stone / Peter Dazeley 11bl; Taxi / Paul Viant

31fclb; The Agency Collection / Rubberball Productions 32br; Workbook Stock / Jay P. Morgan 37tl. **NHPA / Photoshot:** Stephen Dalton 19fcra, 19fcr. **Photolibrary:** 39bl (kids); Age Fotostock / Jack Milchanowski 26cla; Garden Picture Library / Hemant Jariwala 40fcla; Juniors Bildarchiv 27fcr; Peter Arnold Images / Kelvin Aitken 35br; Peter Arnold, Inc. / John Cancalosi 21cra. **Royal Tyrrell Museum / Alberta Tourism, Parks, Recreation and Culture:** Wolfgang Kaehler 21br. Science Photo Library: Richard Bizley 39clb (ichthyosaurs); Christian Darkin 38bc.

Jacket images: *Front:* **Corbis:** Bob King tl. Fotolia: Cantor Pannatto bc. *Back:* **Dorling Kindersley:** Robert L. Braun - modelmaker fcl; Graham High at Centaur Studios - modelmaker c (brachiosaurus); Jeremy Hunt at Centaur Studios - modelmaker fcr; Paignton Zoo, Devon cr.

All other images © Dorling Kindersley
For further information see: www.dkimages.com